D0708259

THE FUTURE OF MODERN POLICING

1981 Edition

The Team at Fenchurch East. Hard as nails.

THE FUTURE OF MODERN POLICING
1981 Edition

DCI GENE HUNT

BANTAM PRESS

LONDON · NEW YORK · TORONTO · SYDNEY · AUCKLAND

TRANSWORLD PUBLISHERS
61–63 Uxbridge Road, London W5 5SA
A Random House Group Company
www.rbooks.co.uk

First published in Great Britain in 2008 by Bantam Press
an imprint of Transworld Publishers

ISBN 9780593062036

2 4 6 8 10 9 7 5 3

Based on an original design created by Red Bee Media and unreal design.

Writer: Guy Adams
Designer: Lee Thompson
Commissioning Editor: Sarah Emsley
Editorial Angel: Rebecca Jones

A CIP catalogue record for this book is available
from the British Library.

Addresses for Random House Group Ltd
companies outside the UK can be found at:
www.randomhouse.co.uk
The Random House Group Ltd Reg. No. 954009

The Random House Group Ltd makes every
effort to ensure that the papers used in its books
are made from trees that have been legally sourced
from well-managed and credibly certified forests.
Our paper procurement policy can be found at:
www.randomhouse.co.uk/paper.htm

Typeset in Baskerville & Avant Garde.

Printed and bound in Italy by
Graphicom.

www.kudosfilmandtv.com
www.bbc.co.uk/lifeonmars
www.bbc.co.uk/ashestoashes

▊ CONTENTS

The Guv.

INTRODUCTION

I wrote another book once. I know, shocking, isn't it? I've written more books than I've bloody well read.

My first book was a rule book telling the copper how to do his job. It covered everything from the basics of driving and dress through to the mechanics of an investigation. It also had a beautifully illustrated guide to knacker-slapping in interrogations. It was a work of genius and I have no doubt it saved lives. Probably cost a few too but there you go. You don't make a steak pie without gutting a few heifers.

Unfortunately that book no longer does everything a guide to policing should. It was written back in 1973. Eight years ago; eight of the *longest*, *weirdest*, most *changeable* years you can imagine. Looking back at it now, 1973 seems like a different planet.

Technological development has become unstoppable, world politics is as mad (and irritating) as a basket of ferrets playing castanets and some days it seems the rules change as often as a high-class hooker's underwear.

It didn't help transferring to London from God's Own Earth of Manchester (I ran out of people to slap there). This certainly is the City of Red Tape and you need to know how to weave your way through it.

So, has the job got easier with all these leaps forward? Don't be soft, it's more difficult now than it ever was.

Think of the classic Wild West sheriff, stood on his own in the middle of Main Street, facing off a gang of vicious outlaws with nothing but his six-shooter and his wits to rely on. He's mad to take them on but if *he* doesn't then nobody will... and that just won't do at all.

That's a good metaphor for policing.

If you swap the gang of vicious outlaws for an army of chainsaw-wielding Brixton boys with the full tactical support of twelve Sherman tanks and a field full of Trident missiles.

Pointing right at your head.

BOOM

That's policing nowadays.

So, you would be forgiven for thinking the police need to be given *more* leeway rather than less when it comes to combatting the slimy bastards that want to kill us all in our beds.

You *might* think that.

Thing is, these days the copper is treated as if he is just as much a villain as... well, the bloody *villains*. All you have to do is turn on the TV or pick up a newspaper to see someone laying into us. Accusing us of extreme violence, of trumping up charges, of looking after number one and doing whatever it takes to secure a conviction.

Once upon a time that was the bloody job description.

'Sorry, m'lud, for using "extreme" violence on the nasty psycho in the dock but we felt it necessary so that some poor bastard didn't experience "extreme" murder.'[1] Ridiculous.

Still, I don't make the rules, I'm just here to give you some guidance on how to follow them and still secure a conviction. How to keep the streets clean and hold onto your job. It's a tricky balance, I'll warn you now. There's no room for divs on the force anymore. You need to be able to *think* on your feet, not just kick someone's head in with 'em.

Bollocks!

This book, unlike the last, isn't going to give you the general basics of policing. There's not space for that (that and the fact that I can't be arsed. I want this bugger written before last orders). I'm working on the assumption that you have the training and a little nous. What you don't have – and who can blame you – is a handle on the new attitudes that are flooding the force.

---

1   Not sure what 'extreme' murder would entail. Perhaps digging you back up and machine-gunning you in your coffin. Or nuclear warheads up the bum.

The world's changing faster than Danny La Rue on amphetamines and you want to keep up.

The book is split into two halves: 'home' and 'away'.

That's right, pal, terms you can understand.

'Home' details the changes within the station, the different policies and practices, the way in which you are now expected to go about your job.

'Away' is a breakdown of what's different on the street, the drugs and the politics, the public opinion and how to survive it.

Lots of useful stuff in this pocket-sized portion of the Gene Genie.

Don't think for one moment I trust you just to read and absorb though – the book also has exercises to make sure you've got these pearls of wisdom into your thick heads. So...

Shall we get on with it then?

Gene Hunt

DCI Gene Hunt

Section One
HOME

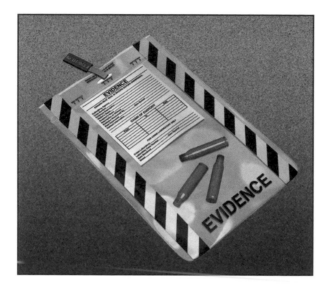

Evidence used to be a dirty word. Like 'scab-whore', 'arseholes' or – my personal favourite – 'shit-biscuit'. It was uttered by journalists, constables and criminal lawyers and had no place on the firm and manly lips of a ranking detective. Now, it's the thing a copper thinks about most.[1]

The due process of law used to be like a ball-cock – it was part of a simple yet effective mechanism for the removal of shit. Now it is a stumbling block: the cling-film across the lavatory pan, the throbbing pile cluster on the ringer of policing.

So, what *is* a copper to do?

First of all, let's define terms. What actually *is* evidence?

It is the unarguable proof that the person we *say* did something actually *did* do that something.

Simple, eh?

---

1   Excluding fanny, we're only human.

No, it's not, actually. Evidence can be a lot more complex than it appears at first glance. You see, there is *good* evidence and *bad* evidence. Good evidence is the sort of proof that will have your slag swinging for it in a court of law. Bad evidence is the sort that will more than likely see you replacing him as the 'accused'. Perhaps it's easier to define evidence by what it's *not*.

Evidence is not:

A) 'I BLOODY KNOW HE DID IT, M'LUD, look at 'im, he's got "guilty bastard" written all over his face.' Gut instinct is vital in policing but gets you precisely nowhere in court.

B) THE STAINED STATEMENT you typed before stepping into the interrogation room. General rule of thumb: the more bloodstains a statement has on it the less admissible it tends to be in court.

C) SOMETHING YOU GET BY BRIBING or threatening as many people as you can so that they will swear blind they saw your suspect doing whatever it is you're accusing him of.

Solicitors – like this one – will have you over a barrel if your evidence isn't up to scratch.

D) A LITTLE 'EXTRA SOMETHING' you can add to your investigation just to impress the boss. It's vital. You need it. Like oxygen. Or beer.

eh?

So, how do you get this elusive 'evidence' then?

Well, luckily there's lots of ways you can gather enough to get your case through court. Let's look at some of the most common methods:

A) A SIGNED CONFESSION. Now, remember: a signed confession is worth *nothing* unless you can show it was given voluntarily rather than through a thorough knowledge of the pain centres in a suspect's body. Yes... the suspect has to actually *want* to say he did it and sign a legally binding document confirming the fact. This is obviously extremely unlikely. *Extremely*. About as likely as Debbie Harry sitting on your face and screaming, 'Guess my weight, big nose.' So let's start looking at realistic possibilities, shall we?

B) RELIABLE EYEWITNESSES. By reliable I of course mean 'not a nutcase dancing up and down the office scribbling his statement using his own sticky arse-pies'. You can't just grab *anyone*. Ask the Queen Mum if she clocked anything first. If she was elsewhere then set your sights lower.

This is not the way to present a confession.

C) **FORENSICS.** We'll have a whole section on these white-coated nutters later but the things they can do these days make your mind split in half. They can get dabs off eyeballs for Christ's sake! Eyeballs!

D) **AN ANCIENT METHOD USED BY DETECTIVES** since the dawn of time: *investigating*. I know it's a radical idea but just do your best job and try to uncover the facts.

Now, given how precious evidence is, it's not always just lying around for you to trip over.[2] It has to be hunted out. Here are some common places evidence can be found:

A) THE RUBBISH BIN. People throw all sorts of stuff out and you can find out a lot about a man by the contents of his black bin bags. For instance, if you emptied a bin sack of 40 empty Fray Bentos pie tins and three blow-up dolls – all with punctures – what do you immediately know about the occupant? Eh? Yes! He's a fat bastard with a high sex drive but no girlfriend. He's also a div who needs to learn that going on top with his lard mass is not the way forward with inflatables.

B) THE CAR. People are less careful what they leave lying around their car than they are their home. Check the floor, the boot, the ashtrays... If they have a stick-on Garfield, what does that tell you? Yes, they're a Grade A Twat. Full marks. Book 'em for something. *Anything*.

C) CHECK THEIR KEYS. Do they have locker keys? It's getting worryingly popular these days for curly-haired poofs to join

---

2   Although I do know an officer who twisted his ankle once stumbling over a bloody chainsaw left at a murder scene.

a local gym to 'work out'.[3] Once upon a
time if a bloke needed exercise he bought
a dog or parked the car a street away
from the boozer. We are living in sad
times. Anyway, if he has a locker he may
have thought it was a safe place to hide
something important.

D) PLACE OF WORK. Check his office, his
judge's chamber, his workman's shed,
wherever it is he hangs about when he's
clocked on.

If nothing else, checking in all the above places
will guarantee you find his special stash of porn.
Thank the Lord nobody's suggested a bloke
copping a free glance at some prime gusset is
politically incorrect. There are some freedoms
left.

---

3   Let me see if I can 'work out' how much of a tosser they are.
Hmm. Hang on, I'm thinking. Oh yes, of course, it's 200%
Fur-Lined, Ocean-Going TOSSER. Makes you sick.
Unless it's a ladies gym and they need someone to wipe the
exercise-bike seats clean. Where's me chamois?

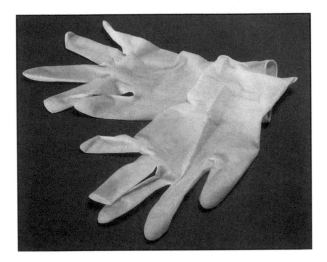

Handling and Presentation

Evidence is so important to a modern copper that it has its own rules with regards to its storage and presentation. The worry is that some cack-handed, bacon-butty-eating, fag-smoking wassock will contaminate the evidence with his dirty mitts.

You called?

Follow the simple Hunt guide to safe contact:

Handling evidence is a lot like having sex with someone you just met: wash before and after and make sure all important areas are encased in rubber.

That'll see you right.

In *both* situations.

Taped Evidence

Weird, I know, but I always tape interviews. It's a habit I got into back in the early seventies and the tapes can be a valuable source of evidence. Most people are thick, their statements will be contradictory, and they will give themselves away just by the things they say.

True story: I once interrogated a bloke connected with a Post Office blag. 'I never did it,' he tells me, 'I've never even been to Crouch End.' I tell him that the woman behind the counter remembers him clearly as he was flirting with her. 'Liar!' he shouts. 'She was Ginger. I have got *some* bloody standards.'[4]

---

4   I personally have nothing against our Ginger-haired brethren. Ginger-haired ladies work *much* harder in bed than most. Of course, they *have* to, but still, worth bearing in mind, eh?

Super Skelton's paperwork avoidance excuses:
1) The Dog ate it
2) I left it on the bus
3) I did do it and it was really good but then I was attacked by a team of crack ninjas and it got damaged in the arterial spray as I whipped their yellow arses.

1.2 PAPERWORK

Sometimes this is the most ridiculous job in the world, filled with methods and complications that make you wonder if it wasn't designed to help crime rather than stop it.

Paperwork's evil. We know that. Still, it has become fashionable amongst the higher ranks to expect extensive and legible documentation for every bloody thing we do.

Nowhere is this more prominent than in the art of report writing.

Not only do our superiors wish for plenty of detail but they also prefer a rather formal tone when compared with the style of old.

Here, for example, is a fairly standard report from ten years ago:

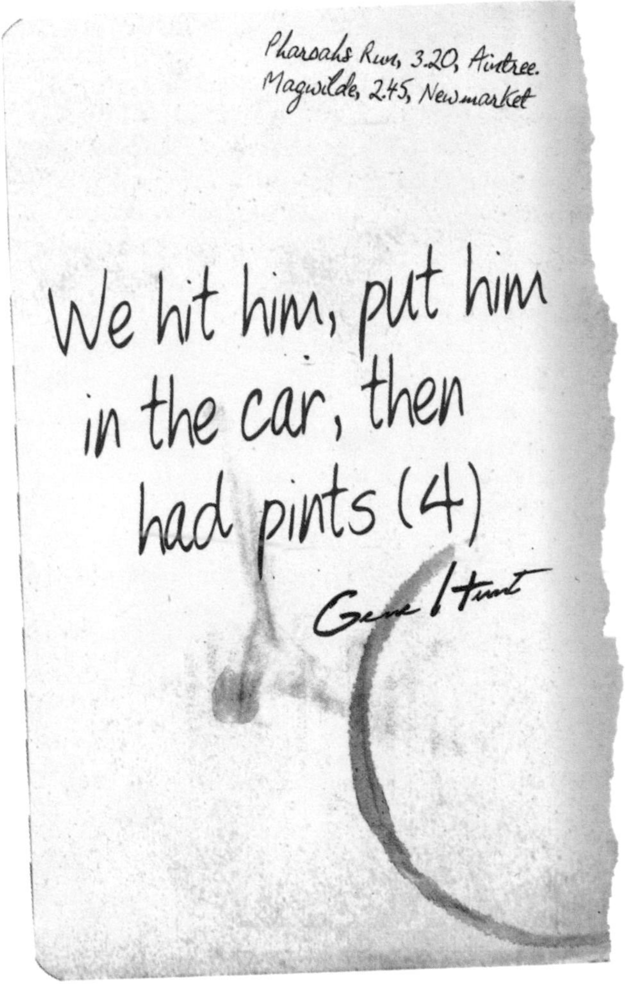

Pharoahs Run, 3.20, Aintree.
Magwilde, 2.45, Newmarket

We hit him, put him
in the car, then
had pints (4)

Gene Hunt

This sort of document is now deemed completely unsuitable.

Picky gits.

Here is a textbook example of how a report should be written. Note the obsessive detail and the use of big words when simpler ones would do just fine:

```
Name: DCI Gene Hunt
Badge Number: 000123
Division: Fenchurch East C.I.D.
Crime Number: 00000069
Date: 18/08/81

I was heading south-easterly along
the corridor of division headquarters
when I noticed a distinctly
pronounced trembling sensation
emanating from my gastric area.
When taking into due consideration
the Asian comestibles and hop-based
libations I had consumed the night
before, I could only come to the
conclusion that nature was taking its
course.

Proceeding with careful haste towards
the fourth-floor water closets I was
relieved to note that I was able to
touch posterior to plastic in time
to avoid any unnecessary stainage of
division carpet tiles.
```

I paid particular attention to the
illuminating graffito found on the
Formica-surfaced reverse of the
lavatorial stall. It showed a most
interesting level of anatomical
detail regarding the union betwixt
DS Ray Carling and the rectum of a
Labrador.

**See what pointless turns of phrase I come up with
to make it sound more hoity toity? They love that,
do the brass.**

**It can also be bloody useful in 'tidying up' certain
events that may have occurred during the course
of your investigation. Here's a few particularly
choice examples lifted from past reports:**

Detective Chief Inspector Hunt was
greatly startled when the suspect
stumbled and collided with him. DCI
Hunt appreciates that the slight
grazing to his knuckles that resulted
from the collision is – while
unfortunate – a worthwhile sacrifice
of his person in the pursuit of
justice.

DCI Hunt considers himself extremely
lucky not to have fallen down the
stairwell himself as the reports of

all present clearly state he made a grab for the suspect several times in an attempt to stop his descent.

DCI Hunt would have done anything to maintain his cover at that point and the complaints from the ladies of the Streatham WI regarding both his language and genital exposure show that he was successful.

Play your cards right and you can turn a dismissal into a commendation.

Me, with medals. Yes, they're mine. Camera never lies, does it?

An Equal Opportunity Piss-taker.

1.3 POLITICAL CORRECTNESS

Is there another phrase as likely to really piss us coppers off as 'political correctness'?[1] As soon as you say it it makes every bastard in the room groan and start shouting the most offensive things they can think of – and, believe me, in my nick that's *pretty* offensive.

Now, don't get me wrong, like most people I can see that certain things are out of order and we shouldn't condone them. Racism, for example. It may surprise you Southern ponces but I've never had anything against our friends from across the water. *Any* water. Whatever your skin colour you're welcome, just bring some of that food with you as my guts can't get enough.

Especially curry. How can *anyone* dislike a nation that invented curry? They wear those turbans to keep the bloody genius in, I tell you.

Still, that doesn't mean I won't tell a joke every now and then that some would say is politically incorrect.

I will also tell a joke about the English. The Northerners. The Southerners. I am an equal opportunity piss-taker.

---

1   Aside from 'Time at the bar, please' or, 'No, I don't like doing that, it's *dirty*.'

WDI Bolly Knickers.

Doesn't mean I wouldn't get great pleasure out of slapping one of those skinhead National Front tossers, though. I would. And *have*.

Sexism, there's another. Now, I'm not even a *bit* sexist. I'd say girls can do lots of things *better* than men. Cleaning, cooking, oral sex. They're a talented bunch are the ladies.

In fact, I am proud to say that I am personally responsible for a major piece of sexual equality within the Metropolitan Police. It was me that invented the bottom stamping for new female recruits. This is where a freshly inked rubber stamp is applied to the female buttocks in a ceremony of great solemnity. And yes, before you say anything, it *is* equality because once we blokes have seen *their* arse we show them *ours*. See? *Equality*.

Still, political correctness is the way of the future and I'll tell you now: it'll come to no good. The more you say you can't do something, the more people will want to do it.

Here are some practical pointers for keeping your nose clean, most particularly when dealing with the press (who will jump down your bastard throat for the wrong word before you can say 'Bernard Manning').

1. **AVOID ANY FORM OF RACIAL ADDRESS.**
   It's safest and easiest. Today's 'black' is tomorrow's 'coloured'. They move the goalposts when you're not looking. Seriously, it's like a secret password, who knows what you're allowed to call somebody at any given moment? Maybe there's a newsletter and they just forget to deliver mine, I don't know.

2. **KNOW YOUR BUTTOCKS.**
   Gone are the days when you could give a passing female rear a friendly slap. I mourned their passing like the death of an old friend. Now you can look but not touch – like a starving man in a field of fine rump steak. Unless it's someone you know, of course,[2] in which case get in there.

3. **KNOW THE LINGO.**
   It's not just racism and sexism, political correctness covers those poor sods that have some form of physical or mental handicap too. If there's one thing I won't stand for in my department it's people using slang terms for the disadvantaged.[3] You will use the correct, scientific name at all times, you will call them *spastics*.

---

2   By which I mean you're on speaking terms, y'know, you actually know their name.
3   That and not standing your round.

Political Correctness – The Future

You don't need me to tell you that all this is madder than Toyah's hairdresser on a windy day. The only time anyone should even say 'PC' is when they're wondering who's nicked all the best biscuits from the station canteen.

What we have here, rather than something that protects 'civil freedoms' (choosing your own tie, watching John Wayne, pissing in the open air… all the things we enjoy on a day-to-day basis), is something that will soon have us absolutely terrified to open our mouths.

You mark my words, this is going to get worse and worse until, down the line, you won't be able to understand a word people are saying to you. Give it five years and talking will be like trying to shovel spunk with a fork: hard work and likely to see you locked up if done in public.

But then I'm not the sort of bloke to say offensive things so maybe I'm just missing the point.

Forensics – still can't identify a div, though, can it?

It used to be that if you found a dead body you whipped it down the morgue, popped a thermometer up its arse with one hand and ate your lunch with the other. You had a stab at guessing the time of death and then went for a pint.

Now they've turned it into a bloody science.

There are several distinct areas:

1. **CRIME SCENE**
    As mentioned in the 'evidence' section, the movement of detectives at crime scenes is now thoroughly regulated so as to avoid contamination of evidence. You mustn't touch stuff, basically.

    That's down to the forensics boys who ponce about in their white suits poking guts into bags.

    What a shame. Nothing I would love more than getting up to the elbow in some dead bugger's cavities (although you get up to twenty years for that, I believe).

2. POST MORTEM

Or necrophilia as most would call it. This is where the coroner takes the stiff apart to find out what happened. Sometimes this is extremely useful, sometimes it is just sick lab kink (if the bloke has a hatchet sticking out of his face I don't need his kidneys weighing to give me cause of death, do I?).

Outside of these obvious moments, there are times when the information the coroner can provide beggars belief:

a) Judging the height of the attacker in stab cases by the angle of knife entry.

b) Telling whether the killer was right or left handed.

c) Grabbing an image of the killer's face by wiring up a television to the victim's brain and recording the last thing they saw.[1]

You wouldn't want to share your lunch with 'em but there's no doubt a coroner's worth his weight in pork pies when it comes to an investigation.

---

1   Alright, they can't actually do that one yet but I saw it in a film once and it was *brilliant*.

3. **LAB WORK**

This is where the real geeks live, messing about with their test tubes and bunsen burners. Through 'toxicology' not only can they tell whether someone's been poisoned or not but they can also tell whether the victim has had alcohol recently[2] or taken drugs.

They also analyse the victim's stomach contents.

---

2   I assumed that meant in the last half hour or so but apparently it stays in the bloodstream for *hours*. I don't think I'd have been able to give a clear reading since I was six.

I'll say that again, shall I? They analyse the victim's *stomach contents*.

Disgusting bastards...

> *''Ere Derek, look at this, what do you think it is?'*
> *'Bit of potato, maybe? Swede? Difficult to tell with dead man's belly soup, innit?'*
> *'Like nailing broth to the wall. I'll say potato. What about this?'*
> *'Jesus... an eyeball? Some kind of fruit? Lot of carrots, aren't there?'*
> *'Stomach lining.'*
> *'Eh?'*
> *'That's pieces of stomach lining.'*
> *'Oh. **Tastes** like carrots.'*

Urggghhh.

Now, all of these departments – despite the fact that they are obviously staffed by sicko mentals – are there to make your life easier. Give 'em everything they need to do their job and they'll make yours a hell of a lot easier.

Additional Notes

Still, despite having made it clear that the mad bus called 'forensics' should only be driven by those funny-smelling science-types that have trained in it, there are some peripheral uses that the canny detective should be aware of:

A) **THE MORGUE CONTAINS A CONSIDERABLE AMOUNT OF COLD-STORAGE.** This can be of particular use/ interest to the lager enthusiast who wishes to keep his Hofmeister cool. Lager and a fridge, the best combination since someone first threw a slice of pig at a frying pan.

B) **THE MORGUE IS ALSO A GREAT SOURCE OF COMEDY GIFTS FOR LEAVING PARTIES.** Why waste good cash on getting a man an embarrassing blow-up doll when the real thing can be had on free loan? Bear in mind all parts are for 'show' only, and don't prop the buggers up near any radiators.

C) **SAVE ON DOG FOOD.**

D) **THE HOME-BREWER CAN FIND MUCH OF INTEREST IN THE LAB,** though some combinations are liable to leave you blind, convulsing or dead. Much like German wines.

E) **IT'S NOT UNHEARD OF FOR FORENSICS TO OFFER A 'FREELANCE' SERVICE.** A good friend of mine soon solved the mystery of the 'happy wife' using the combination of a used bed sheet, an empty shot glass and a tame DNA technician. He's now happily divorced and will not be talking to his brother anytime soon.

Pong Rules!

Now, I come from an age when technology to a policeman was a set of handcuffs. Walkie-talkies were whistle-shaped and your 'Civilian-Interaction Liaison' was constructed out of wood and made a satisfying sound when you clobbered someone on the nut with it.

All of it did its job. It didn't need plugging in. You didn't have to work your way through a manual the size of a phonebook trying to understand the German for 'how does this bastard thing switch on?'[1]

Things have changed.

You can't move for extra kit these days, it feels like *Tomorrow's World* have moved into the bloody office. If you're into that sort of thing, it's a dream come true. *yup!*

But then you've never touched a woman and your mummy dresses you funny so shut it, geek boy. *Oi!*

---

1   Not that a real man reads instructions, of course. We just smack the thing until it either does what we say or breaks beyond repair. Either is fair play to us.

Whatever your feelings, you're going to get nowhere in this job unless you at least *try* and make a go of understanding the gubbins they dump on your desk, so here's a quick look at the more obvious technical devices you're likely to stumble across, if only when you bust the door down of your local fence:

1. **VCR**

    Not, as I first suspected, a medical term for Delhi-Belly (Very Creamy Runs) or even the shortened but always worthwhile advice we've all heard at one time or another (Virgins Cling Rigidly). A 'VCR' is in fact a Video Cassette Recorder.

    That's right, gents, now you can tape *Grandstand* while you're down the pub. Forget what I said before, technology's a beautiful thing.

It looks a bit like Frankenstein's Toaster[2] with a big tray on top that pops out at the flick of a switch (with a gentle click that may remind some of the bay doors opening on a bomber plane). You load the videotape in, close it up and press Play, simple as that.

Due to their high ticket price these are becoming popular haul items, which means three things:

a) Don't be surprised if your local Rumbelows gets its display window smashed in on a weekly basis.

b) You should be able to get yourself one if you keep your eye on the evidence room.

c) It's not just about new stuff to nick either, the specialist porn market has been quick to catch on. These VCRs look set to be as popular as the eight-track and the smut-hounds are eager to supply.

---

2   Do NOT put bread in there, it will not toast. I know this, I was *very* drunk and *very* hungry. The VCR is now *very* broken.

2. **Personal Cassette Player**
   Another common item in the swag bag:

Disadvantages:
   a) Ignorant bastards can't hear a word
      you're saying as they're mainlining their
      KC and the Sunshine Band.

   b) The second-hand sound of the music is
      loud enough to be irritating but too quiet
      to be identifiable.

Advantages:
   a) The means with which to strangle the
      bastard user is dangling conveniently
      near their throat.

   b) The cassette player is the perfect
      combination of size and weight to be
      thrown a great distance with minimum
      effort.

3. **CAR PHONE**

New toy for lazy bastards with money. The clue is in the title. Car. Phone. For people so desperate to speak to someone that they can't wait until they either get home or see a phone box.

No doubt someone will invent the Zeltron 2000 Arse Scratcher for them any moment.

Given how expensive this rich man's bauble is, it's still a relatively rare sight on the black market.

It's also annoyingly hard to tap calls placed on it (without hiding in the glove box, say).

On the plus side, it's a nice plastic club for twatting the driver with if they give you aggro for pulling them over.

4. **DESK COMPUTER**
The 'future' of policing.

Yeah, *right*.

Still, let's have a blow-by-blow account of
how to operate such a thing. I have employed
two different methods and I will give you the
breakdown of each.

Croft Digger – 4.00pm Newmarket
Reynolds Runner – 2.30pm Walthamstow Dogs

Option One:

A) GETTING STARTED

How do you turn it on? Simple. You
march out of the office and grab the
first spotty twat who looks like he knows
about computers. You drag him in front
of the thing and then make him do it.

B) THE WAIT

You now hang around waiting for the
damn thing to actually do something.
This is the point when I most feel the
little sod is laughing at me.

C) THE RESULT

You use the arrow keys to control the
straight line and stop the stupid little
ball from getting past you. It's like
tennis, you see, but without the short
skirts or strawberries. They call it Pong.
A word that immediately brings another
to mind: shit.

Option Two:

A) LEAVE IT SWITCHED OFF and use the bastard
as a paperweight.

Option Two is, of course, the sensible man's
choice.

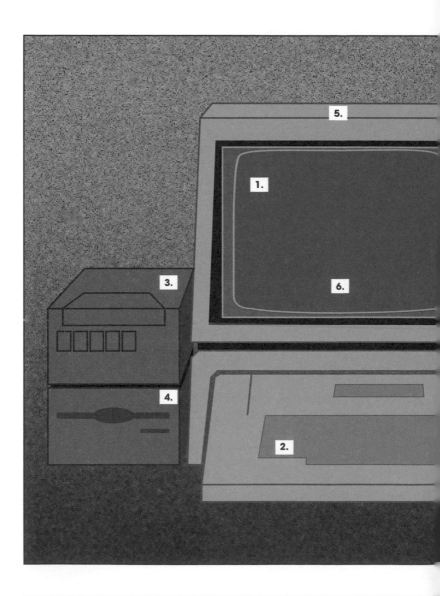

1. **MONITOR:** Like a small TV that doesn't show programmes. Which is a bit like a cheap whisky that doesn't get you drunk.

2. **KEYBOARD:** Operated with both index fingers and powered by swearing. This is the device where the operator is able to make the computer do what he wants. In this sense it is very much like a man trying to steer angry bulls with the aid of a small leek.

3. **CASSETTE DRIVE:** When you play a cassette in here, the noise is a high-pitched, brain-melting screech that makes you want to dig your own ears out with a pen. This effect can be achieved using a normal cassette player and the latest Leo Sayer album.

4. **FLOPPY DISK DRIVE:** I smacked the person who first told me what this was called.

5. **TOP OF CASING:** Coffee mug storage platform.

6. **EXTRA OBSERVATIONS:** After hundreds of years proving that the human eye responds best to plain black writing on a white background the tossers over at Boffin Central went for tiny green neon on a black screen. This combined with the awkwardness of using Tipp-Ex (fine if viewed at precisely the right angle but useless otherwise) means that a computer's sod-all use for writing stuff.

Section 1a – Evidence

1. **After a spate of gruesome murders, police are called to the home of Timothy Lebbon. Lebbon is quite clearly mad as a bucket full of frogs on heroin. The neighbours say he watches his 'video nasties' at full volume at 'all hours', they hear the sound of electric saws and – sometimes – 'so many dogs barking you'd think someone had set fire to Battersea'. None of these obvious signposts to Nutter Castle means a thing, though. You need *evidence*! Here is an excerpt from his taped statement. Underline and note down anything suspicious.**

LEBBON: I never did nothing. I couldn't kill loads of people and eat their meats like it was fine fillet steak (*Lebbon makes sound like a gleeful pig snorting Vicks*). <u>It's just not in my nature.</u>

INVESTIGATING OFFICER: For the record, Lebbon, we are talking to you in regards to several complaints

of disturbing the peace, nobody's
mentioned murder. Yet.

LEBBON: Just saying.

INVESTIGATING OFFICER: Now that
you've brought the subject up,
though, do you recognise any of these
people? (*IO lays down photographs of
the victims.*)

LEBBON: I don't know anybody. At all.
Never have.

INVESTIGATING OFFICER: Please look at
the photographs.

LEBBON barks like a dog.

INVESTIGATING OFFICER: For the
record, Timothy Lebbon is licking the
photographs of the murder victims.

LEBBON: Just seeing if they're
familiar. I would remember her I'm
sure, she's quite fatty. I'm hungry
now, can I have something to eat?

INVESTIGATING OFFICER: Something
tells me we might be here for a while
I'm afraid. You can eat later.

LEBBON: Hungry NOW!

INVESTIGATING OFFICER: You'll eat
LATER, pal!

*There is the sound of a scuffle
followed by a scream from the
INVESTIGATING OFFICER.*

INVESTIGATING OFFICER: For the bloody
record, Lebbon's trying to eat my
bastard arm!

Your Answer

I think it is very suspicious how Lebbon (like the singer?) wants to eat policemen. I think it is very suspicious that he makes pig noises. He says he doesn't know anybody, that must be a lie as everybody knows somebody (like your Mum or something).

Basically I think his real name is Billy Nutjob and he lives at Madder House, Crazy Lane, Loopytown, Barking.

I also think Timothy is a girl's name. Maybe that's why he kills?

2. Here is an artist's sketch of Lebbon's front room. Make a note of all items you would wish to bag as evidence.

Your Answer

I would collect:

* The basket of feet and that.
* The sauce bottle (in case it wasn't sauce

    but gut juice).
* Jars of parts (including arse in a

    bottle as that's actually a bit of a laugh).
* Axe and knifes.
* Chainsaw Physco Poster 'cos it's really rare!

Section 1b – Paperwork

Turn the following into a polished report that not only satisfies the need for detail but also presents the events in a way that won't cost you your job:

1. You are pursuing a suspect in a robbery case. In order to successfully restrain him you whack him over the head with a dustbin lid and make him eat the contents of a used nappy as he's made you bloody furious.

Your Answer

The suspect fought to escape capture despite several attempts at explaining that we was only wishing to talk at him. It was during one of his particularly energetic breaks for freedom that he caught the rubbish containment tin with his foot causing the steel encasement hat to fly up and collide with his visage. As I tried my most hardest to administer medical aiding I made an impromptuous decision to use a baby's seat bag as a rudimentarian smelling salt. This was extremely successful and I probably saved his life. Thanks.

2. *You spot a really nice gold wristwatch in evidence and decide it would be a waste to leave it on the metal shelving to gather dust. Popping it on your wrist, you go about your day.*

   Later on you are attending a press conference organised by the Chief Commissioner when he clocks your new watch.

   During the live broadcast he announces the watch is his, that it was part of the evidence for a break-in suffered at his home, dropped by the burglars as he chased them.

Your Answer

Having been informed regarding the regrettable burlgary of the noble Cheif Commissioner in his homestead I made a mental decision to do everything within my considered powerfulness to secure the return of his worldy goods and parafanalia. Realising the press and media confrontation was an ideal opportunity to spring my trap on the insideyous perpetrators by being clearly seen wearing the watchpiece, I was completely unswerved in expecting the robberising swine to get in touch with thoughts of blackmail and then I would secure them using my cunningness.

And Kung Fu.

3. *You're asked to bodyguard an attractive young Russian model who is due to testify against mobsters.*[1]

During the course of the day it becomes obvious that she's attracted to you.[2]

Finally you give in to your urges and have sex in the back seat of your car.

During climax you are knocked out by sneaky Russian assassins. When you wake up you are still inside the Russian model – though she is dead – and surrounded by a group of Girl Guides.[3]

---

[1] Shut up, could happen.
[2] Also extremely possible, if not downright likely.
[3] Yeah ... stretching it a bit, I'll accept that. It's always what happens when I dream it, though.

Your Answer

~~Fuck...~~

~~I~~ never meant to...

During the course of guarding the life of Natalya Vodkashosticumtwitch I was, at all times, most circumstitious with regards her continued safety. The attack came when I fell completely sleepified due to what must have been poison in some of the Ribena I had been ~~drin~~ imbibing. When I woke up it was to find what I guesed must be the unconscious body of ~~my~~ her. Deciding that it was likely due to the same poisonification that had affected me, I fell back on my Territorial training and tried to poke the poison out.

Section 1c – Political Correctness

Describe the following in a politically correct fashion:

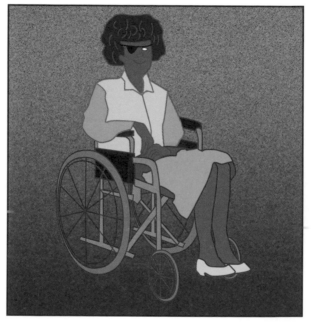

Your Answer

~~Ironside~~

Um... she's a ~~pirate~~ sat down person with hair.

Calling a Spade a Spade

All of the following have been turned into absolute gibberish by political correctness. See if you can figure out what is being described:

a) Financially Induced Slit Vendor

Prostitute

b) Vertically Compact Princess Lover

Dwarf

c) Amber-follicled Freckle Transporter

Ginger

d) Wool-loving Mutton Piercer

Sheep Shagger

e) Rectally Active Theatre Lover

Larry Grayson

Section 1d – Forensics

1. You arrive at a crime scene to find a blood-soaked room and a man lying in the middle of the floor. He's got gaping knife wounds all over him. Next to the body is a knife. It is most likely the murder weapon and could provide all the evidence your case will need when it goes to court. Detail the steps you would take to secure the knife as evidence.

Your Answer

I would get someone else to pick it up

so as not to contaminate the evidence.

I'd tell them to put it in a bag.

2. Take an educated guess as to how the following people died:

Victim A – Cause of Death:
1. Poisoning
2. Suffocation
3. His head, for Christ's sake! Look! His head!!

Victim B – Cause of Death:
1. Old age
2. Drowning
3. The 9.24 to Colchester

Victim C – Cause of Death:
1. Heart attack
2. Leprosy
3. Jaws

Section 1e - Technology

How would you use the following?

 To record or play films such as 'Fist of Fury', or 'Enter the Dragon'.

 To listen to the top 40 recorded off the radio.

 To play Pong!!

 To shoot the next person who says Pong's shit!

This was a trick question. If you answered the top three correctly you were supposed to use the last one to shoot yourself, you sad git.

Section Two
AWAY

Pope Lennon says
"Imagine there's no heaven..."

So, you think policing has changed a lot in the last few years? That's *nothing*. The world *outside* the station's four walls changes more often than the batteries in Thatcher's vibrator.

Just look at the things that have happened over the last few months:

The septics went and put Ronald Reagan in power! It'll be John Inman for Prime Minister next.

I'm free!
Vote for Me!

At least someone had the good sense to try and assassinate him within a couple of months. It's a pity that, like all Americans, the shooter had lousy aim.

It seems assassination (or at least attempted assassination) is a popular sport this year. Pope John Paul Ringo[1] copped one. Some bugger made us think the Queen was for it at the Trooping of the Royal Colour.[2] Thankfully, much like the Chief Commissioner (or so the wall in the Gents tells me), he was firing blanks.

---

1   Or whatever his name is.
2   Always a thrill. *I'd* shoot someone if I had to sit through it.

France has decided to abandon capital punishment. Strangely, after seeing our entry in the Eurovision this year I was very much of a mind that we should bring it back. I would never have imagined my response to seeing two blondes have their skirts ripped off would be to sign out the shooters and march on Dublin to catch them as they left the show.

Cheryl Baker, she's dirty!!!

The Tories, in their considered wisdom, responded to an economic recession by increasing taxes. We've had three assassination attempts this year, room for one more, surely. I'll teach that bastard Geoffrey Howe to up the price of my fags. Still, I suppose they can't go up *much* more...

Maybe I should complain to Ken Livingstone now he's taken control of the Greater London Council. Perhaps he'll subsidise fags for the workers. Something tells me I'll have to be quick. The way Red Ken flaps that gob of his I can't see him running things in London long.

'But what's all this got to do with being a copper, DCI Hunt, sir?' you ask.

Everything.

What's going on in the world shapes the *people* in that world. It's just as vital you know your way

Bucks Fizz. Never has skirt removal been so horrid.

around current affairs as it is the back streets
of your manor. Culture too. If you want to
understand people, we're told, understand their
culture. Their music, books, fashion.

Politics in particular changes the way people are,
the way they'll kick off, they way they'll behave.
You think the Budget isn't going to nudge a few
more people to pop down their local bank with a
shotgun? Of *course* it bloody is.

Also, you have to play the game. Watching the way
the dust clouds settle in the House of Lords is
no different to studying form for Aintree. These
crusty buggers hold our future in their hands.

What are the major threats facing the country right now?

1. **TAKING THE MICK**

    When I was a kid an Irishman was a dozy buffoon who reeked of Guinness and shredded shamrock. He was the thick one in all the really good jokes.

    Now they're trying to bomb us.

    Some say there's a connection, can't see it myself.

    Can't believe I've just come across as sympathetic to the Irish... not like me.

    Still, as most of 'em are too thick to read they'll never bloody know, will they?

2. CIVIL UNREST

I don't know, seems you can't say or do
anything on a housing estate these days
without someone reaching for the breeze
blocks or matches.

Anyone would think they didn't like living in
concrete shitholes. Something they'll have to
get used to if 'Major Threat' number three has
her way...

3. THE BALL SHRINKER
Was the ENTIRE country drunk on Election Day?

4. Terrorism

Everybody's obsessed with it. Whether it's the IRA or Iran, it keeps Joe Public in a panic.

When you've been through the sort of divorce *I* have, there's no such thing as terror any more (actually, sod the divorce, the divorce was easy. The marriage, that was the really terrifying thing).

But then I'm the Manc Lion. I've been scientifically proven to be 200% harder than you soft Southern poofs.

Yes, the world's getting to be an even more dangerous place, but, you know what? Don't bother putting your helmet on of a morning unless you're prepared for some nasty bastard to try and knock it off before lunchtime.

We're police officers, getting in a ruckus is part of the job.[3]

On the subject of which:

---

3   Or, in the case of the Iranian Embassy last year: 'We're police officers, making sure the gun-toting bastards were well served with sandwiches and fags while clocking Kate Adie's manly and rather disappointing arse is part of the job.'

5. RIOTS

Not very many months ago, we had a bit of a set to in Brixton. Those lovely creatures on the top floors once again decided it was time for them to earn their living and come up with some new ideas. They came up with *Operation Swamp 81*. This involved sending constables into Brixton – where they are much loved – and grabbing any passing strangers they thought looked 'a bit suspicious'.

Now, I can only assume the good folk of Brixton were in a bad mood that day as a goodly bunch of them took issue with this and before you know it there's cars, buildings and *people* on fire.[4] The fire brigade refused to set foot in the area until the morning and it took a thousand officers to bring things under control.

Now, I don't intend to go into whether or not the riots should have started in the first place – as I said before, know your current affairs, know your world, you start to see these things coming – but:

Don't moan about having to do your job. Again, if you'd served with me in Manchester and seen City fans kick off (*after* the kick off... if you see what I mean), the Brixton riots would have felt like just another Saturday when the ref was blind.

You can see already that the riots are going to be used by the politicians as a big stick to beat the police force with.

In our defence – not that we should bloody need one – I will explain slowly the mechanics of a fight.

Are you sitting comfortably? Then I shall begin.

---

4   Alright, it was a bit more complicated than that but I wouldn't want to beat lovely Lord Scarman to dishing up all the 'facts', now would I?

Jim has spotted PC Bill
A man he'd like to beat and kill

PC Bill has been told by his Big Boss to go to the Magical Kingdom of Brixton. Once there he should ask everyone he sees to empty their pockets.

Jim LIVES in the Magical Kingdom of Brixton. Jim doesn't WANT to empty his pockets.

Jim is feeling grumpy because the Magical Kingdom of Brixton is as beautiful as the inside of a goat and his wife has been going on and on and on...

Jim suddenly realises he HAS got something in his pockets he would like to show PC Bill. He has a pair of fists. He will show these to the officer with great pleasure. Over and over again.

*Jim thinks he'll use this plank of wood
It smashes more than knuckles could*

Jim spots a lovely plank of wood. 'Hello!' he
thinks. 'I bet I could do some good thrashing
with that!'

PC Bill doesn't enjoy having his face filled with
planks. PC Bill has a plan:

'I'll smack him first,' thinks PC Bill
'Smack him till he stays quite still!'

PC Bill won't be having Jim's plank wrapped around his head today. PC Bill has given Jim a sound twatting with his truncheon instead!

No fun for Jim of course but he'd have done the same. If he'd been quicker.

But wait! Who's this? A naughty man
He cracks Bill's skull as fast as he can

Jim's friend, Derek, WAS quicker and has now removed some of naughty PC Bill's teeth using high-speed wood-to-face action.

Derek is very happy in his heart. He thinks he's got away with smacking PC Bill.

PC BILL'S FRIENDS ARRIVE

'Oh dear, oh dear,' the riot squad cry,
'Now seven shades of shit will fly!'

But Derek didn't realise PC Bill had also got some
friends: PC Andy and PC Jeff! Now lots of people
want to fight!

Everybody started punching everybody else. Soon
you couldn't move for the spray of teeth and the
sound of cricket bat on brain.

So, you see? Riots start small but before you know it it's every man for himself. A man has to do a fair bit of damage just to keep his head on his shoulders.

It's a little unfair to suggest the police aren't allowed to do their share of the smacking, isn't it? What are they supposed to do? Roll over and take a beating?

The first punch is to be avoided for as long as possible as once it's thrown plenty more will follow. Sometimes these things never quite kick off. They can just be two big gangs shouting about which of them has the biggest dicks.[5]

Keep your eye on each other's backs. If you're all looking out for one another you've a better chance of leaving with a head that has a little less breeze block in it than it could have done.

Oh and one last point, you soft Southern bastards: standing at the back may be safer but nobody's going to thank you for it. *Get in there*.

---

5   Not literally, of course. That would be a night at the Heaven nightclub. So I'm told anyway...

DI Carling, Licensed to be a Daft Twat in a Tux.

6. I SPY
As a final note on the subject of politics:

Governments are playing dirtier than ever. A couple of years ago we had a Bulgarian killed by an *umbrella* here in London. Not in the sort of hard, messy and tiring way you imagine either, a poisoned dart was injected from the tip!

What's next? Dead Russians in the trees, fired from ejector seats?

Skeletons with the distinctive bite-marks of piranha fish dumped by the roadside?

Jet-pack explosions?

Politicians. Governments. Spies.

We're the police, we don't move in the circles of international espionage. The name's Hunt, not Bond.[6]

Still, I don't see why I should turn a blind eye to them playing silly buggers with their microfilms and exploding thumbnails. I bloody hate spooks.

Spies are arrogant, flashy, high on their own sense of self-importance and completely uninterested in whether they step on the public's toes as they go about their business. Other than that we have sod all in common.

We live in confusing times.

If you haven't got a headache at the end of your shift, you weren't doing it properly.

---

6   I could take him any day. I have the perfect special gadget for it: the Gene Hunt Fistmatic 4000. In seconds it can turn from a normal-looking hand to something perfectly suited to sparking out white-jacketed ponces.

     I'd then book him for being ripped to the tits on a girl's drink and spend a lovely night in the cells with him, sniffing his fingers and hoping it was Ursula Andress.

I was an Ovaltiney!

People will do anything to get high these days. If someone said you could get a buzz off the smell of old haddock, Barbara Woodhouse would be knickerless in seconds.

The youth of today, eh?

Of course, when we were teenagers the choices were a little more limited. And rubbing Horlicks on your gums did get boring after a while.

Still, at least that meant we just poured beer down our necks and smoked fags until we puked.

Nothing that could kill you, in other words.

But then we used to meet at youth clubs or village halls. They weren't the sort of place you really got carried away in. Carried 'out of' when you'd necked too much of the cooking sherry you'd half-inched from home, yeah, but no, never carried 'away in'.

These days the club scene is what these bright young things love. Maybe it's because it's dark enough in there that the spotty bastards might pull. Surely it can't be the bloody *music*.

The Bloody Youth of Today

Ridiculous, aren't they? Eh? I mean, what do they look like?

Sad fact: you are bound to come into contact with these bright young things in the course of your duty. So here is Hunt's guide to the 'look' of eighties youth:

1. *HAIR: Built high with chemicals that would make the men of Porton Down weep with fear. Still, one advantage is that the entire head is now both as ridiculous-looking and as flammable as an otter swimming in a petrol tank with a sparkler up its arse. Now… where's me matches?*

2. *MAKEUP: The only time you should see this much makeup on a man is when you're burying him. What does the big girl look like, eh? There's a reason some people call makeup 'slap'.*

3. *OUTFIT: Only a blind man goes out like this in public.*

4. *OUTFIT: More lace than Mae West's knicker drawer.*

5. *SKIRT: If it wasn't for the pulse (and likely the flapping gob) you would be forgiven for thinking you were looking at one of those horrible dolls old ladies use to cover their bog rolls.*

6. *WHITE DENIM: You're as likely to see me in white denim as foreskin pie on the menu at a bar mitzvah.*

Now, usually when these idiots get dressed up it's to go to one of their horrible 'clubs'. While there they will take drugs that delicately smash the brain out through the eyes.

I'll share with you the contents of a recently distributed memo about the more popular recreational drugs. Second thoughts, it's boring as hell, I'll paraphrase a little:

Marijuana/Pot/Cannabis/Whatever

The old ones are the best, eh? At least you can have fun with potheads and say you'll give 'em a head-start before you arrest them. I usually make it half an hour or so. They tend to have got to their feet by then.

Either that or just walk back to the car leaving a trail of Mars Bars, if you fancy a lazy afternoon. The sad bastards will follow it all the way onto the back seat.

Cocaine

Cocaine has almost exactly the opposite effect
on the user to pot. It packs the buggers full of
energy, confidence and a gob that won't stay shut.
Considering the cost of the drug it's used almost
exclusively by business and media types. Yes,
that's right, just the sort of tossers you could well
do *without* having shouting in your face.

Often 'cut' with other white powder – baking
powder, for example – to make sales more
profitable, it is, as yet, impossible to cut the drug
with 'punches to the face'. But I'm working on it.

Cocaine is usually sniffed. Excessive use can damage the inside of the nose, rot the lot off and leave the daft sod with a single big nostril. That weeps.

So it's not all bad news.

There is also a new form known as 'crack' cocaine which is starting to appear. It's cheaper (due to its impure nature) but the effect when smoked can be much stronger.

For those that found cocaine too, y'know, *wishy-washy*.

A common sign of the crack user is that their lips will be burned and chapped from the hot end of the glass pipe they use to smoke the stuff.

That and the fact they'll be standing in the middle of the road, bollocks out, screaming at ghosts.

The crack addict is not subtle. I dare say most of you would know one when you saw one.

On the subject of which:

Heroin

You'll know a heroin user easily enough. He'll be the emaciated dead thing you fell over after entering his flat. That's him... yes... the grey smelly one, yes... the one that's going *runny*.

Heroin is a recreational drug in just the same way that licking a whirring bandsaw is recreational carpentry.

Heroin and cocaine can be combined in one injection (a 'speedball').

Or, if users prefer, they can take the safer and cheaper route of trying to catch and kill rabid dogs with their teeth.

PCP (phenylcyclohexylpiperidine)

Nothing quite like a drug that makes a good chunk of takers want to kill themselves due to the horrible hallucinations it can cause, is there? Not something you'd see someone trying to market outside the narcotics field.

'The new Ford Christ! Sends fifty per cent of drivers piling into a tree on test drive.'

'The Breville ToasterMax 2000, now with the ability to burn your eyes out of your sockets while you wait.'

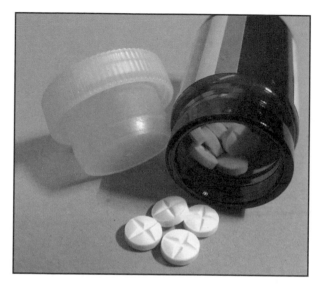

Barbiturates

Barbiturates act on the central nervous system...
blah blah... science, science, depressants... here
we go:

Users describe the following symptoms:
relaxation, increased sociability, good-humour,
intoxication, loss of inhibitions.

Really? It would seem I am a frequent user of
barbiturates. I prefer them in their affordable
pint-glass form.

LSD (Lysergic acid diethylamide)
Makes the purple custard of the Lootytwits burst
its banks and flow down Jellythwack hill covering
everything in frumptious oils and crinkly eye-gas
as it passes.

If we're lucky the glistening newts of the sun's
last dreaming will lap it up with their fiery
tongues of righteousness and everyone in the
garden will be free.

Prince Bumblejack of Frazzlelube Castle prays
this will be so and has unfurled his brilliant arse
feathers in anticipation of flying his warm gut
winds to the land of his true love.

Practical Advice

It's not just the buying and selling of drugs that's the problem. It's the knock-on effect of the entire industry that makes our job difficult.

In order to fund their habit, addicts will often turn to other crimes. Facing a smack addict with a shotgun is about as fun as juggling with dog diarrhoea. It can only be a matter of time before he starts shooting at the pixies he can see dancing around your face.

When forced to deal with addicts or dealers you must always remember the Gene Hunt Method: Silly Prats Like It Frigging Fierce, or SPLIFF.

Basically slap them until they stay slapped.

In this sense drug-related crimes are one of the easier areas of modern policing.

Now, you know when you're face to face with an addict – the screaming gives it away – but how do you identify a dealer?

Spotting a Dealer
Dealers seem to fixate on four main locations:

A) **HOUSING ESTATES**
Spotting a dealer in residential urban areas is easy as, unlike most predatory animals, he's shit at camouflage. While a tiger or cheetah moves with stealth and blends perfectly into its background, these tossers are poncing around the concrete and graffiti in their Topman suits. He's the only one who looks like he's got money.

B) **'THE CITY' – BUSINESS DISTRICTS**
It's difficult when you're one of those high-flying corporate monkeys (or hanging by your stripy braces in the 'arse eat arse' world of the stock exchange). The stress, the need to stay ahead, the immense pressure of being such a colossal *prick* every waking moment of your worthless life.[1]

To relax, these poor oiled and perfumed turds like nothing more than hurling fistfuls of cocaine up their noses.

---

1   Those helpful yanks have come up with a new word for these tossers, the 'Yuppie'. It stands for 'Young Urban Professional'. Apparently black ones are called 'Buppies' and gay ones 'Guppies'. I say keep it simple and call them all *Cuppies*.

Looking for a dealer in business districts is also simple: he's the only one *not* screaming about how absolutely arse-shatteringly wonderful he is and laughing in such a grating and high-pitched manner you could swear he was being bum-raped by hyenas.

c) NIGHTCLUBS

Now this is a little more difficult. The Oxford Dictionary (probably) defines a nightclub as 'a dark place packed wall to wall with people you want to smack'. How then are you supposed to clock the dealer?

There is a standard Gene Hunt procedure that is simple to follow: shoot everyone in the club and accept that the deaths of some frilly ponces are acceptable collateral for the bagging of a drug dealer. Oh, alright... that's a lie. Keep your eyes out for the exchange of money. That is, after all, what the bastards are there for.

d) SCHOOLS

Get 'em while they're young, eh? Smack any bastard not in short trousers.

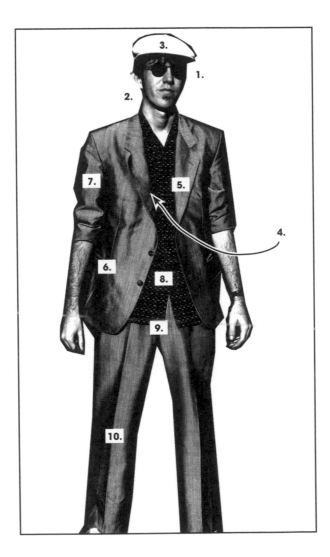

The Anatomy of a Drug Dealer

There are those who believe drug dealers are human, just like us. Not me. Therefore take a little time to familiarise yourself with the anatomical differences I have spotted over the years.

1. *STUPID HAIRSTYLE, the perfect combination of bad taste and pig grease.*
2. *HIS FACE: A certified Gene Hunt 'Punch Zone'.*
3. *EVIL LITTLE BRAIN, the source of all his bad ways. Best smacked out of his nostrils via the firm application of a truncheon to the back of the dealer's skull.*
4. *INSIDE JACKET POCKET: Bulging Wallet Container Vats.*
5. *HEART? Nothing to see here... move along.*
6. *JACKET POCKETS: Drug pits.*
7. *SUIT: So shiny that smelly sewer rats use it as a mirror to comb their hair.*
8. *OVERACTIVE BOWEL NETWORK that has developed into the major bodily organ. Some scientists believe this is through the repeated method of stashing drugs in its stomach for smuggling purposes. Upshot is: the drug dealer is literally full of shit.*
9. *SO SMALL scientists have yet to come up with a way to measure it.*
10. *APPLY SOLE OF FOOT HERE at great speed to make dealer more stationary. And noisy.*

A pillock of the community.

These days it's not enough to catch criminals, we're supposed to skip through the streets playing hopscotch with children and helping old ladies across the road too. Half Clint Eastwood, half Jimmy Bloody Savile... Christ, my head hurts with the confusion sometimes.

Or Bruce Lee! Heeyaaaaaa!!

It started off simple: every now and then we had to send Plod out dressed up as Tufty the Tossing Squirrel[1] or something. It kept the bosses happy and made us look nice. Then they started getting carried away. They wanted ranking officers to visit schools!

The idea of having the police force and the community work closely together is destined to fall on its arse for two very basic reasons:

They hate *us*.
We hate *them*.

---

1 Yes, that is his full name, along with Barry the Bum-Chum Badger and Willy-Waver Weasel. Now grow up.

Let's look at why the above two points are the case:

is it a bird? is it a plane? no, it's super skelton!!!

Why do the Public Hate the Police?

Once upon a time coppers were heroes. Now, telling someone you're on the force is likely to get you in as much trouble as dipping your tadger in the punch at the Royal Garden Party. Our reputation has gone to the wall. *We're* the bloody villains.

The lefties would say that this is because coppers have spent years acting outside the law, intimidating the public with threats of violence and trumped-up charges, extracting confessions through physical and psychological torture, lining their own pockets with bribe money and siding with the criminal when it was in their best interests to do so. Bollocks. We were doing that for years and nobody cared.

The reason the public hate us is that they think they could do *better*.

They are *wrong*.

Obviously.

Why do the Police Hate the Public?

Because everything that's wrong with being a copper is the fault of the public. If they're not breaking the law, they're getting under our feet while we try and catch someone who is. Seriously… who wouldn't hate the public? They're as irritating as thrush but with half the intelligence.

Still, our bosses will have us jumping through hoops to try and create a better impression. This is because they live in an imaginary world on the top floor[2] and do not have any knowledge of how the *real* world works. Unfortunately we now have to play along with their dribbling schemes in order to keep our jobs.

---

2   'Commissioner's Castle' it's called. All day brightly coloured elves dance around hurling golden prize medals at their puffy masters, drenching them in port and clapping as they make finely tailored suits from the skins of poor people.

Public Misconceptions

What do the public know? Most coppers would weigh in with the answer 'sod all'. Unfortunately it's worse than that. The public are *packed* full of information, the problem is they got it from *television*. In Joe Public's air-filled, spaz-factory of a mind I spend most of my day hanging around with Bergerac and Juliet Bleeding Bravo.[3]

This means that I can solve crimes in an hour (depending on adverts), fall in love with some silly bint every week and – most importantly – come up against villains that can't shoot straight, cover their tracks so badly Helen Keller could find 'em with a peg on her nose and all too often have a soft side to their character – they're good folk, just brought up on the 'wrong side of the tracks'.

---

3   Or maybe that Jill Gascoigne off *The Gentle Touch*, much nicer than that Bravo Rug Muncher.

I met a crook with a heart once. He kept it in his pocket and tried to eat it once I had him cornered.

TV is made up. The public don't understand that. This is because the public are *thick*.

Which is certainly why the next little idea should have been stamped on before the politicians got hold of it:

Neighbourhood Watch

For those of you not familiar, a bit of background: this is an initiative the suits upstairs have nicked from America. It was given a trial in Chicago and deemed a success.[4] It is a scheme whereby the public are encouraged to police *themselves*. If they see something suspicious they are encouraged to monitor and report their findings to their local police station.

This is, of course, a bloody *stupid* idea.

We're going to spend half our time rescuing dotty old pensioners who've had a case of the Miss Marples, going after street gangs with nothing but their colostomy bags for defence.

I bet we won't be allowed to use rubber bullets on 'em either.

---

4   Much in the same way as the septics considered the Vietnam War to be a success.

We, in turn, are to maintain a high level of contact with the locally nominated co-ordinators of the Neighbourhood Watch schemes, informing them of current crime trends and generally keeping them abreast of OUR BLOODY JOB.

This plan is to be given a trial in the small village of Mollington, Cheshire next year.

I'll say that again. THE SMALL VILLAGE OF MOLLINGTON, CHESHIRE.

If it turns out to be a highly successful method of cutting down sheep-fiddling and cheese theft we can expect it to be implemented nationwide thereafter.

In case there's any doubt in your mind, let me predict precisely how this is going to work out:

Location: A Police Station. The telephone rings. The Neighbourhood Watch co-ordinator sighs and drinks some more vodka, half a bottle or so, just enough to get through the call.

CO-ORDINATOR: (Picks up phone) What?

MAD OLD THING: I've got 'im!

CO-ORDINATOR: Who?

MAD OLD THING: That crazed killer I told

 you about, the one with the mad hair and eyes like the devil!

CO-ORDINATOR: (Sighs again, it's almost impossible to move he's so depressed, he decides he'll probably top himself when he finishes the call, just to give him something to look forward to.) The one who hasn't actually done anything?

MAD OLD THING: It's only a matter of time, young man! It's obvious just to look at him. He's evil!

CO-ORDINATOR: (Who knows exactly who he thinks is evil - this crazed old sow and the high-ranking bastards that made it his job to deal with her.) You say you've 'got' him, what does that mean exactly?

MAD OLD THING: Don't worry, lad, I stove his face in with a poker, just like all the others, there'll be no crazy folk slaughtering innocents here, not on my watch!

CO-ORDINATOR drains the vodka and starts clubbing himself to death with the bottle.

Mad, completely unworkable and pointless. For those precise reasons I expect it to be nationwide within three years.

Keep 'Em Peeled

While we're on the subject of television, I will
mention my strongly felt belief that good coppers
make just as worthwhile TV stars as we would
expect TV stars to make coppers. The two trades
are mutually exclusive.

When some poor bastard's been taken hostage
and everybody's pulling out the stops to secure
their safe return, you'll find it's rare that the Met
would call on, say, Little and Large to help out.
Cannon and Ball have never assisted with any of
our investigations, nor are Les Dennis and Dustin
Gee on the payroll in an advisory capacity.

Why then is it deemed a good idea for me to go on telly and sit next to Shaw Taylor for five minutes? They don't even like it if you tell jokes.[5]

Which is not to say it can't sometimes be useful to have the media help with an investigation. Sometimes you want the public 'on side' or you just need to buy yourself some time to get on with the job. Just don't go on telly yourself, you'll only end up looking like a tosser. Leave it to the pros and hope they show you the same courtesy.

How to Handle the Public

Having said all that then, how *is* a bloke to talk to them?

Simple rule of thumb here: imagine this member of the public is just like you or me.[6] If you were to come up to me, stick your middle finger up and call me a toss-bucket, it's *extremely* likely you're going to get a sound battering. You will receive this battering as you've pissed me off by being rude. The public are just the same. Except a little more sensitive. Think of 'em all as a bunch of girls and you might just get away with it.

---

5   Which is a shame, because if the producer had let me tell mine about the four nuns and the length of oiled hosepipe the show would have gone down much better.

6   Just not as clever or painfully shaggable.

What's that, young 'un? Eh?
Speak up or I'll think you're not cooperating.

Where's it all goin' then, eh?

Looking at how much the world's changed since I wrote the last book, I dread to think what things are going to be like ten years from now.

Air cars? Spaceships? The Tories still in power?

Perhaps we'll have laser beams built into Plods' helmets. Then they could blast cats from trees or incinerate small children for nicking penny chews from corner shops (scratch that, the only thing you'll be able to chew for a penny come 1991 will be a rat's arse and then only if you ask nicely and promise to take it out afterwards).

Perhaps we'll be policing the streets of England against thought crime? Banging people up when they've only *thought* of doing something criminal. Hope not. I'll be serving a life sentence for sex crimes against Charlie's Angels the minute they turn their mind-reading machine on.

Whatever, you can guarantee it will come with an army of young gits that see it as an excuse to elbow us old pros out of the way. With this in mind, let me give you one last piece of advice:

Fight the bastards until they bury you!

They'll be wiping my arse and reminding me what my name is before they drag me off the force.

Hell, they do that for the Chief Commissioner *now*.

However fast 'progress' marches, the Gene Genie can march faster. I'll see you in the year 2000, you won't be able to miss me: I'll be the flash bastard swooping through the air in my new Audi Rocket Car, with a crew of blaggers hanging off my bumper.

Until next time...

Gene Hunt

EXERCISES

Section 2a – Current Affairs

Which of the following news stories are true?

a) In 1979, on the 18th of February, it snowed for half an hour in the Sahara Desert.

b) Jimmy Carter still lives in a small hut in the White House garden enjoying tea parties with NASA-trained chimps and watching out for nasty rabbits.

c) Popular charity-raiser and spaz Gil Hollis was recently robbed at gunpoint. All of the money he had managed to raise by sitting in cold baked beans for three hundred years was taken by an unnamed gang of thugs who evaded capture.

d) General Pinochet becomes the manager of pop group Bucks Fizz as he 'just loves that cheeky little Cheryl Baker'.

e) Penguins will become extinct within four years due to an increased lust for chocolate biscuits in the western world.

Section 2b - Riot Language

Like many areas of policing today, the language of a riot situation needs altering in order to become 'brass acceptable'.

Take the words on the left and match them up with their translation on the right.

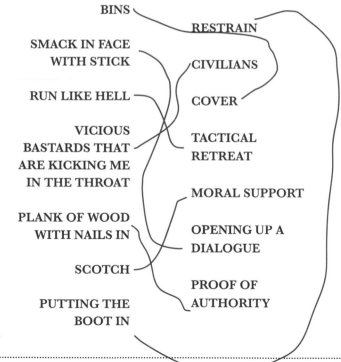

BINS

SMACK IN FACE
WITH STICK

RUN LIKE HELL

VICIOUS
BASTARDS THAT
ARE KICKING ME
IN THE THROAT

PLANK OF WOOD
WITH NAILS IN

SCOTCH

PUTTING THE
BOOT IN

RESTRAIN

CIVILIANS

COVER

TACTICAL
RETREAT

MORAL SUPPORT

OPENING UP A
DIALOGUE

PROOF OF
AUTHORITY

Section 2c – The Big Wide World

1. Know Your Drugs:

   You arrest a bunch of Silly Little Bastards in a nightclub, they're all ripped to the tits on one thing or another – know enough of the signs to guess what they're on? Let's see:

   a) The Kid is hyper and won't shut up, is it:
      - Cocaine
      - Emsley's Puff
      - Dover's Powder
      - Whippets

   b) He's pointing at things dancing in the sky and laughing like a twat, is it:
      - Gusset
      - Beck's Dots
      - LSD
      - Rod Hull

   c) He's asleep, is it:
      - Leper's Pieces
      - Marijuana
      - Felch
      - Libblefister

2. A mad nutjob's on the loose. Construct a specialist team from the following in order to solve the case:
    - JOHN 'BERGERAC' NETTLES
    - THAT BLOKE OFF QUINCY
    - OFFICER DIBBLE
    - DAME EDNA EVERAGE
    - WEE JIMMY KRANKIE
    - SHERLOCK HOLMES
    - ME, THE GENE GENIE
    - SHAW TAYLOR
    - DENNIS WATERMAN
    - DANGERMOUSE
    - MOIRA STEWART
    - NORMAN COLLIER

3. Select the best forms of address for use when interacting with members of the public:
    - SHITLUMPS
    - FAT COW
    - ARSEFACE
    - BUMCHUFFER
    - YOU
    - SIR   *all of them!*
    - SLAG
    - MADAM
    - FLAPS
    - GONAD
    - WETBRAIN
    - WANKSTAIN

4. Spot the Drug Dealer

a) A playground

b) An urban estate

c) The woods

d) Behind a waterfall

Across

1. What a copper thinks about more than anything else (5)
4. Scum in a suit (4,6)
5. Bracelets (9)
8. Ambrosia (6,4)
12. Place to keep your beer cold (6)
14. A hell of pens and long words (9)
15. I love biscuits, me! Ooh, where's me pencil? (4)
16. My best friend (or so the public thinks) (8)
19. Plastic paperweight, filled with wires and shit (8)

Down

1. Pastime of necrophiliacs and whackos (9)
2. Utter Div (5,7)
3. City of Dreams (10)
6. Double-O PONCE (5,4)
7. Bane of my life (8)
9. Me (3)
10. Whether it's mine or Suzi there's nothing I like to get in to more (6)
11. Armed robber (7)
13. Civil Interaction Pole (9)
17. Method of keeping fit (4)
18. Fiery stew of kings (5)

Answers

1c (page 65)
a) Prostitute or sex worker
b) Dwarf
c) Ginger
d) Sheep shagger
e) Any famous bum-bandit

1d Question 2 (pages 67 and 68)
'3' for all of them. Obviously. If you
got them wrong then you'll die of
Huntitis when I catch you.

1e (page 69)
This was a trick question. If you
answered the top three correctly –
and let's be honest you know if you
have – then you were supposed to
use the last one to kill yourself, you
sad git.

2a (page 118)
The Sahara one. Bet that wins you a
pub quiz one day.

2b (page 119)
Bins = Cover
Smack in face = Opening a dialogue
Run like hell = Tactical retreat
Vicious bastards = Civilians
Plank of wood = Proof of authority
Scotch = Moral support
Putting the boot in = Restrain

2c Question 1 (page 120)
Can't remember. If you see someone
selling any of them then give 'em a
smack, just to be on the safe side.

2c Question 2 (page 121)
If you picked anyone other than me
I'll have Keith Harris stick his hand
up your arse and wave you around in
front of the Queen at the next Royal
Variety.

2c Question 3 (page 121)
If you didn't stick to just 'sir' or
'madam' I need you to go down to
Brixton and shout the others at the
first person you see. That should stop
you making the same mistake again.

Crossword
Across:
1.   Fanny
4.   Drug dealer
5.   Handcuffs
8.   Single malt
12.   Morgue
14.   Paperwork
15.   Plod
16.   Bergerac
19.   Computer

Down:
1.   Forensics
2.   Chris Skelton
3.   Manchester
6.   James Bond
7.   Evidence
9.   Guv (God will also do)
10.   Quatro
11.   Blagger
13.   Truncheon
17.   Riot
18.   Curry

ABOUT THE AUTHOR

DCI Gene Hunt transferred from North West District CID to the Met in order to sort you soft Southern poofs out.

Consider yourselves lucky.

Signs of gratitude should be left on his desk (unless said items are so obviously 'hot' they're likely to leave scorch marks, in which case leave, well-wrapped, inside the cistern of cubicle four, third floor Gents).

'Anything you say will be taken down, ripped up and shoved down your scrawny little throat until you choke to death.'

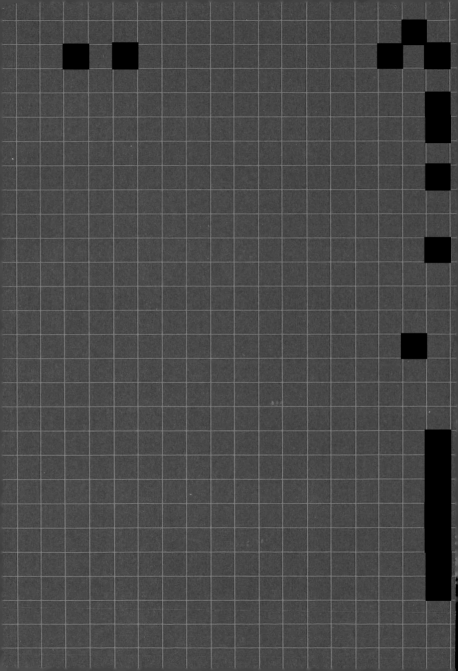